States

INDIANA

by Angie Swanson

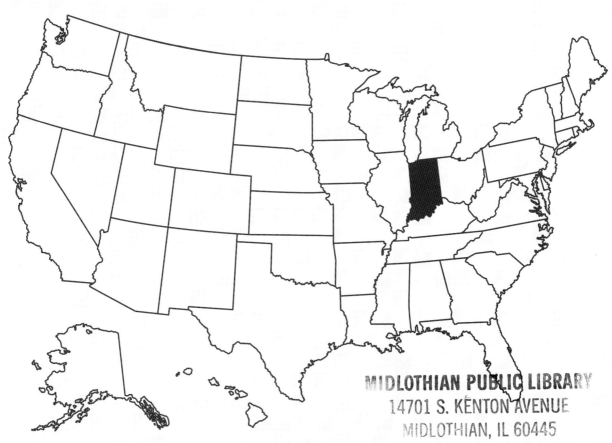

CAPSTONE PRESS
a capstone imprint

Next Page Books are published by Capstone Press,
1710 Roe Crest Drive, North Mankato, Minnesota 56003
www.mycapstone.com

Library of Congress Cataloging-in-Publication Data
Cataloging-in-publication information is on file with the Library of
Congress.
ISBN 978-1-5157-0401-0 (library binding)
ISBN 978-1-5157-0460-7 (paperback)
ISBN 978-1-5157-0512-3 (ebook PDF)

Editorial Credits
Jaclyn Jaycox, editor; Kazuko Collins and Katy LaVigne, designers;
Morgan Walters, media researcher; Laura Manthe, production specialist

Photo Credits
Alamy: Everett Collection Historical, 28; Capstone Press: Angi Gahler,
map 4, 7; Dreamstime: Carrienelson1, top 19, Susan Sheldon, 17; Getty
Images: DEA / G. DAGLI ORT, 25, DEA PICTURE LIBRARY, 12, Vince
Bucci, middle 19; Glow Images: Superstock, 10; iStockphoto: ilbusca,
26; Library of Congress Prints and Photographs Division Washington,
D.C., middle 18, bottom 18; Newscom: akg-images, bottom 19, Andre
Jenny Stock Connection Worldwide, 11, KEVIN LAMARQUE/REUTERS,
top 18; One Mile Up, Inc., flag, seal 22–23; Shutterstock: Aeypix, 6,
Alexander Raths, 14, Alexey Stiop, middle 21, 29, Bryan Busovicki,
cover, carroteater, 9, Connie Barr, bottom left 20, cristalvi, top left 20,
DnDavis, 16, Everett Historical, 27, humbak, bottom right 20, Joseph
Sohm, 5, Kenneth Keifer, 7, bottom left 8, bottom right 8, Michael
C. Gray, bottom 21, Nagel Photography, 13, rick seeney, bottom 24,
Sopotnicki, 15, Tobias Ott, top 21, Victoria V. Ratnikova, top right 20,
www.BillionPhotos.com, top 24

All design elements by Shutterstock

Printed and bound in China.
0316/CA21600187
012016   009436F16

TABLE OF CONTENTS

Want to take your research further? Ask your librarian if your school subscribes to PebbleGo Next. If so, when you see this helpful symbol throughout the book, log onto www.pebblegonext.com for bonus downloads and information.

LOCATION

Indiana is one of America's Midwest states. It's located in the north-central United States. Indiana is also one of the Great Lakes states. A small part of northern Indiana borders Lake Michigan. The state of Michigan forms the rest of Indiana's northern border. To the east is Ohio, and to the west is Illinois. On the south, across the Ohio River, is Kentucky. Indianapolis, the state capital, lies along the White River in central Indiana. Indianapolis, Fort Wayne, and Evansville are the state's biggest cities.

PebbleGo Next Bonus! To print and label your own map, go to www.pebblegonext.com and search keywords:

IN MAP

In addition to being Indiana's largest city, Indianapolis is the second-largest city in the Midwest.

GEOGRAPHY

Indiana has three main land regions. They are the Great Lakes Plains, the Till Plains, and the Southern Hills and Lowlands. Northern Indiana is part of the Great Lakes Plains. Indiana's largest natural lake, Lake Wawasee, is found here. South-central Indiana is called the Southern Hills and Lowlands, while central Indiana is called the Till Plains. Indiana's highest point, Hoosier Hill, is in the eastern Till Plains. It is 1,257 feet (383 meters) above sea level. The Wabash River is Indiana's longest river. It flows across northern Indiana, and then forms Indiana's border with Illinois.

PebbleGo Next Bonus! To watch a video about Lake Michigan, go to www.pebblegonext.com and search keywords:

IN VIDEO

Brown County State Park is in the southern part of the state in the Southern Hills and Lowlands.

Lake Michigan

Tippecanoe River

Lake Wawasee

GREAT LAKES PLAINS

Wabash River

Legend

▲ Highest Point

⬭ Lake

〰 River

TILL PLAINS

Hoosier Hill ▲

White River

Monroe Reservoir

SOUTHERN HILLS

Ohio River

Scale
Miles
0   20   40   60   80
0   20   40   60   80   100
Kilometers

McCormick's Creek State Park offers a variety of recreational activities, such as hiking, fishing, and horseback riding.

WEATHER

Indiana has warm summers and cool winters. The average summer temperature is 73 degrees Fahrenheit (23 degrees Celsius). The average winter temperature is 30°F (-1°C).

Average High and Low Temperatures (Richmond, IN)

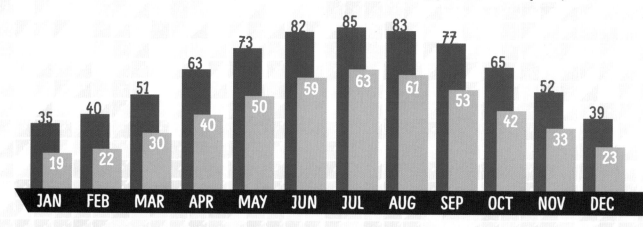

	JAN	FEB	MAR	APR	MAY	JUN	JUL	AUG	SEP	OCT	NOV	DEC
High	35	40	51	63	73	82	85	83	77	65	52	39
Low	19	22	30	40	50	59	63	61	53	42	33	23

Indianapolis Motor Speedway

The Indianapolis Motor Speedway is home to the Indy 500, the world's most famous car race. The Indy 500 is held on Memorial Day weekend. About 400,000 people attend the event. Millions of TV viewers watch around the world.

Angel Mounds State Historic Site

Angel Mounds in Evansville is one of the best-preserved prehistoric American Indian sites in North America. Located on the Ohio River in southwest Indiana, the site was home to Mississippian Indians more than 1,000 years ago. Visitors can explore reconstructed buildings as they learn about American Indian culture.

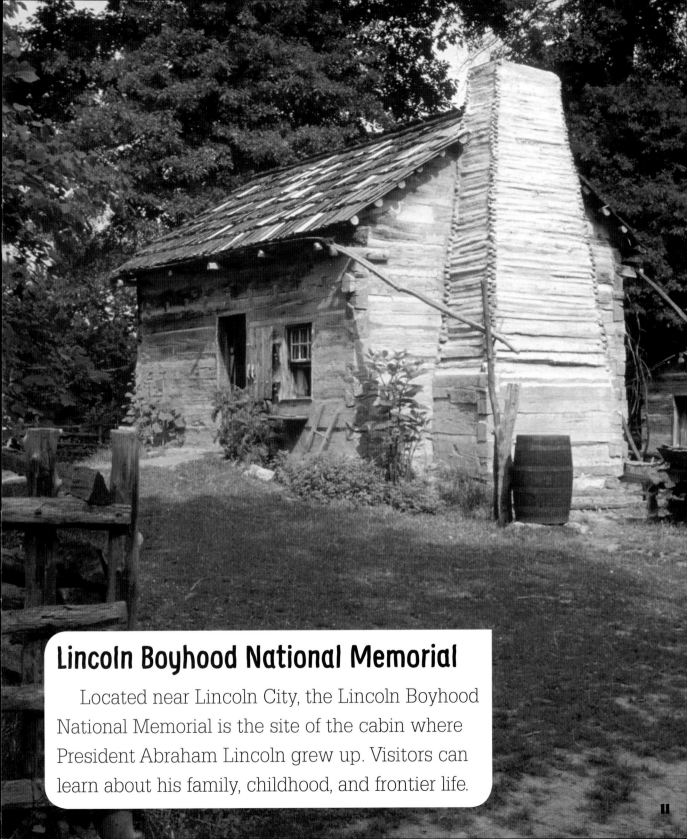

Lincoln Boyhood National Memorial

Located near Lincoln City, the Lincoln Boyhood National Memorial is the site of the cabin where President Abraham Lincoln grew up. Visitors can learn about his family, childhood, and frontier life.

René-Robert Cavelier explored the Great Lakes region in 1679, including Indiana.

Around AD 1000 Mississippian Indians arrived in Indiana. The Miami Indians moved into the area between 1100 and 1300. Other tribes in Indiana were the Delaware, Shawnee, and Kickapoo. In 1679 French explorer René-Robert Cavelier, known as Sieur de La Salle, became the first European in Indiana. In 1763 Great Britain gained the Indiana region from France after winning the French and Indian War. In 1787 the U.S. Congress established the Northwest Territory, which included Indiana. Indiana Territory was created in 1800. In 1816 Indiana became the 19th U.S. state.

Indiana's state government has three branches. The governor leads the executive branch, which carries out laws. The legislature is made up of the 50-member Senate and the 100-member House of Representatives. They make the laws for Indiana. Judges and their courts make up the judicial branch. They uphold the laws.

Indiana's state capitol building is located in Indianapolis.

INDUSTRY

Farming, manufacturing, mining, and service industries are important to Indiana's economy. Corn and soybeans together make up about 50 percent of Indiana's farm income. Farmers in the state also grow hay, wheat, popcorn, fruits, and vegetables. Indiana is a leading producer of hogs, turkeys, and eggs.

Manufacturing is a large part of Indiana's economy. Factories make steel, iron, transportation equipment, food products, wood products, chemicals, and medicine. Indiana is also the largest steel manufacturer in the country. Coal makes up about 50 percent of Indiana's mining income. The state also mines limestone, sand, and gravel.

Indiana is the fifth-largest pork producer in the United States.

More than three out of every four Indiana workers hold a service job. Some work in stores, hospitals, banks, or repair shops. Others teach school, drive trucks, or build houses.

The Indianapolis Power and Light Company provides service to more than 480,000 customers.

POPULATION

With more than 5 million white residents, the majority of Indiana's people have European backgrounds. Many early immigrants were Irish and German. In the late 1800s and early 1900s, many people from eastern European countries such as Russia and Poland came to Indiana. Many of them worked in the steel mills of Gary. African-Americans also worked there. Today more than one-half million African-Americans live in Indiana. Gary and Indianapolis still have the largest populations of African-Americans in the state.

Population by Ethnicity

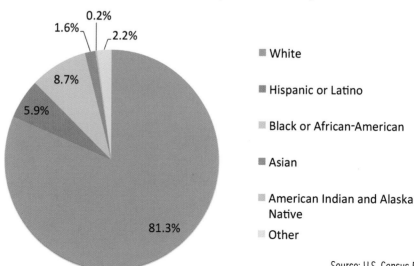

0.2%
1.6%
2.2%
8.7%
5.9%
81.3%

- White
- Hispanic or Latino
- Black or African-American
- Asian
- American Indian and Alaska Native
- Other

Source: U.S. Census Bureau.

Indiana is also home to nearly 400,000 Hispanics. Large populations of Hispanics live in Indianapolis, Hammond, and East Chicago. The Amish came to northern Indiana in the late 1830s. This religious group settled near Nappanee.

The annual Valparaiso Popcorn Festival attracts around 50,000 people each year. A parade, live music, and food and craft vendors are all part of the event.

FAMOUS PEOPLE

David Letterman (1947–) is a comedian and talk show host. He hosted the Late Show with David Letterman for over twenty years. He was born in Indianapolis and attended Ball State University in Muncie.

William Henry Harrison (1773–1841) was Indiana Territory's first governor (1800–1812). Harrison and his soldiers defeated the American Indians in the Battle of Tippecanoe (1811). Harrison later became the 9th U.S. president (1841). He was born in Virginia.

Benjamin Harrison (1833–1901) was the 23rd U.S. president (1889–1893). He had a home in Indianapolis. Born in Ohio, he was the grandson of William Henry Harrison, the 9th U.S. president.

Michael Jackson (1958–2009) was a popular singer, dancer, and songwriter. Jackson was known as the "King of Pop." His top hits include *Thriller* (1983), *Bad* (1987), and *Black or White* (1991). He was born in Gary.

Jim Davis (1945–) is a cartoonist from Marion. He created the comic strip "Garfield," which was first published in 1978. Today the comic appears in more than 2,400 newspapers and is read by more than 200 million people.

Cole Porter (1891–1964) wrote many popular songs for musical theater from the 1930s through the 1950s. Porter was born in Peru.

STATE SYMBOLS

Tree
tulip tree (yellow poplar)

Flower
peony

Bird
cardinal

Stone
limestone

PebbleGo Next Bonus! To make a dessert using fruit from one of Indiana's 50 apple orchards, go to www.pebblegonext.com and search keywords: **IN RECIPE**

Poem

"Indiana," by Arthur Franklin Mapes

River

Wabash River

Pie

sugar cream

FAST FACTS

STATEHOOD
1816

CAPITAL ☆
Indianapolis

LARGEST CITY •
Indianapolis

SIZE
35,826 square miles (92,789 square kilometers) land area (2010 U.S. Census Bureau)

POPULATION
6,570,902 (2013 U.S. Census estimate)

STATE NICKNAME
Hoosier State

STATE MOTTO
"The Crossroads of America"

STATE SEAL

Indiana's state seal shows a scene of Indiana's pioneer days. The seal features a woodsman chopping down a tree in the forest and a buffalo jumping over a log. In the background, the sun sets behind a row of mountains. Around the outside of the seal, the year of statehood, 1816, appears along with the words "Seal of the State of Indiana."

PebbleGo Next Bonus! To print and color your own flag, go to www.pebblegonext.com and search keywords:

IN FLAG

STATE FLAG

Indiana's state flag is blue with 19 gold stars around a flaming gold torch. The torch stands for freedom and the light of wisdom and knowledge. The stars symbolize Indiana's position as the 19th state. The word "Indiana" is lettered in gold above the largest star, which represents the state. Thirteen of the stars are arranged in an outer circle to stand for the original 13 colonies. Paul Hadley of Moorseville designed the flag. It was adopted in 1917.

MINING PRODUCTS

coal, limestone, portland cement, petroleum

MANUFACTURED GOODS

chemicals, motor vehicle parts, petroleum and coal products, food products, machinery, computer and electronic equipment

PebbleGo Next Bonus! To learn the lyrics to the state song, go to www.pebblegonext.com and search keywords:

IN SONG

FARM PRODUCTS

corn, soybeans, popcorn, wheat, oats, dairy and beef cattle, chickens, hogs

PROFESSIONAL SPORTS TEAMS

Indiana Firebirds (AFL)
Indiana Pacers (NBA)
Indiana Fever (WNBA)
Indianapolis Colts (NFL)

INDIANA TIMELINE

1000–1450 Mississippian Indians live at the village of Angel Mounds in present-day Evansville.

1620 The Pilgrims establish a colony in the New World in present-day Massachusetts.

1679 French explorer René-Robert Cavelier, known as Sieur de La Salle, becomes the first European to reach Indiana.

1732 French settlers found Vincennes, the first permanent settlement in Indiana.

1763 Great Britain claims the Indiana region from France after winning the French and Indian War.

1787 U.S. Congress establishes the Northwest Territory, which includes Indiana.

1800 Indiana Territory is created out of the Northwest Territory. Vincennes, in southern Indiana, is the capital.

1811 American Indians fight to keep their lands after Indiana Territory is created. William Henry Harrison, governor of Indiana Territory, and about 900 soldiers defeat several American Indian tribes at the Battle of Tippecanoe near Lafayette.

1816 Indiana becomes the 19th U.S. state. Young Abraham Lincoln and his family move to Indiana, where they will live until 1830.

1825 Indianapolis becomes Indiana's capital.

1841 William Henry Harrison, who served as Indiana Territory's first governor from 1800 to 1812, becomes the 9th U.S. president.

1861–1865 The Union and the Confederacy fight the Civil War. Indiana fights on the Union side. Almost 200,000 Indiana soldiers fight for the Union. More than 24,000 of them die.

1911 The first Indianapolis 500 car races are held at the Indianapolis Motor Speedway.

1914–1918 World War I is fought; the United States enters the war in 1917.

1937

The Ohio River floods, causing many deaths and widespread damage. Jeffersonville, Indiana, located north of Louisville, Kentucky, is 90 percent flooded.

1939–1945

World War II is fought; the United States enters the war in 1941.

1967

Richard Hatcher of Gary becomes the first African-American mayor of a major city.

1989

Dan Quayle of Indiana becomes the U.S. vice president under President George H. W. Bush.

2002 Astronaut David Wolf, an Indiana native, completes his third mission in space.

2012 Tornadoes and storms hit parts of the central and southern United States, causing widespread damage. The tornadoes cause the deaths of 14 people in Indiana.

2014 Governor Mike Pence signs a bill to drop Common Core standards; the state is required to adopt its own educational standards.

2015 A wild black bear is spotted in northern Indiana for the first time in more than 140 years.

Glossary

Amish *(AH-mish)*—a strict religious group that does not use any technological advances from modern times

ethnicity *(ETH-niss-ih-tee)*—a group of people who share the same physical features, beliefs, and backgrounds

executive *(ig-ZE-kyuh-tiv)*—the branch of government that makes sure laws are followed

frontier *(fruhn-TIHR)*—the far edge of a settled area, where few people live

industry *(IN-duh-stree)*—a business which produces a product or provides a service

legislature *(LEJ-iss-lay-chur)*—a group of elected officials who have the power to make or change laws for a country or state

limestone *(LIME-stohn)*—a hard rock used in building; made from the remains of ancient sea creatures

petroleum *(puh-TROH-lee-uhm)*—an oily liquid found below the earth's surface used to make gasoline, heating oil, and many other products

prehistoric *(pree-hi-STOR-ik)*—from a time before history was recorded

region *(REE-juhn)*—a large area

Read More

Ganeri, Anita. *United States of America: A Benjamin Blog and His Inquisitive Dog Guide.* Country Guides. Chicago: Heinemann Raintree, 2015.

Kerzipilski, Kathleen. *Indiana.* It's My State! New York: Cavendish Square Publishing, 2016.

Ransom, Candice. *What's Great About Indiana?* Our Great States. Minneapolis: Lerner Publications, 2015.

Internet Sites

FactHound offers a safe, fun way to find Internet sites related to this book. All of the sites on FactHound have been researched by our staff.

Here's all you do:

Visit *www.facthound.com*

Type in this code: 9781515704010

Super-cool stuff! Check out projects, games and lots more at
www.capstonekids.com

Critical Thinking Using the Common Core

1. Why are there 19 stars on Indiana's flag? (Key Ideas and Details)

2. Indiana's state motto is "The Crossroads of America." If you had to come up with another state motto for Indiana, what would it be and why? (Integration of Knowledge and Ideas)

3. Which ethnicity has the smallest population in Indiana? Use the graph on page 16 for help. (Craft and Structure)

Index